Informing the legislative debate since 1914

Mail and Wire Fraud: A Brief Overview of Federal Criminal Law

Charles Doyle
Senior Specialist in American Public Law

August 6, 2014

Congressional Research Service

7-5700

www.crs.gov

R41930

Summary

It is a federal crime to devise a scheme to defraud another of property, when either mail or wire communications are used in furtherance of the scheme, 18 U.S.C. 1341, 1343. Mail or wire fraud includes schemes to defraud another of honest services, when the scheme involves bribery or a kick back, 18 U.S.C. 1346; *Skilling v. United States*, 561 U.S. 358 (2010). In order to convict, the government must prove beyond a reasonable doubt that the defendant (1) used either mail or wire communications in the foreseeable furtherance, (2) of a scheme to defraud, (3) involving a material deception, (4) with the intent to deprive another of, (5) either property or honest services.

Offenders face the prospect of imprisonment for not more than 20 years, a fine of not more than $250,000 (not more than $500,000 for organizations), an order to pay victim restitution, and the confiscation of any property realized from the offense.

Misconduct that constitutes mail or wire fraud may also constitute a violation of one or more other federal crimes. Principal among these are predicate offense crimes, frauds based on jurisdictional factors other than use of mail or wire communications, and other honest services frauds in the form of bribery or kickbacks. The other federal bribery and kickback offenses include bribery of public officials, federal program bribery, extortion under color of official right, and Medicare/Medicaid kickbacks. Mail and wire fraud are money laundering and racketeering predicate offenses. Numbered among the fraud offenses based on other jurisdiction grounds are the false claims and false statement offenses, bank fraud, health care fraud, securities fraud, and foreign labor contracting fraud.

This report is available in an abridged version as CRS Report R41931, Mail and Wire Fraud: An Abridged Overview of Federal Criminal Law, by Charles Doyle, without the footnotes, appendix, quotation marks, or citations to authority found here. Related CRS reports include CRS Report R40852, Deprivation of Honest Services as a Basis for Federal Mail and Wire Fraud Convictions, by Charles Doyle.

Contents

Appendixes

Contacts

Introduction

The federal mail and wire fraud statutes outlaw schemes to defraud that involve the use of mail or wire communications.[1] Both condemn fraudulent conduct that may also come within the reach of other federal criminal statutes. Both may serve as racketeering and money laundering predicate offenses. Both are punishable by imprisonment for not more than 20 years; for not more than 30 years, if the victim is a financial institution or the offense is committed in the context of major disaster or emergency. Both entitle their victims to restitution. Both may result in the forfeiture of property.

Background

The mail fraud statute was first enacted in the late nineteenth century in order to prevent city slickers from using the mail to cheat guileless country folks.[2] But for penalty increases and amendments calculated to confirm its breath, the prohibition has come down to us essentially unchanged.[3] Speaking in 1987, the Supreme Court noted that "the last substantive amendment to the statute ... was the codification of the holding of *Durland* ... in 1909 [that is, (*Durland v. United States*, 161 U.S. 306 (1896)(rejecting the argument that the statute was limited to the common law crime of false pretenses)].[4] Congress did amend it thereafter to confirm that the statute and the wire fraud statute reached schemes to defraud another of the right to honest services [5] and to encompass the use of commercial postal carriers.[6]

The wire fraud statute is of more recent vintage. Enacted as part of the Communications Act Amendments of 1952,[7] it was always intended to mirror the provisions of the mail fraud statute.[8]

---

[1] 18 U.S.C. 1341(mail fraud), 1343(wire fraud).

[2] The prohibition was thought necessary "to prevent the frauds which are mostly gotten up in the large cities ... by thieves, forgers, and rapscallions generally, for the purpose of deceiving and fleecing the innocent people in the country," *McNally v. United States*, 483 U.S. 350, 356 (1987), quoting, 43 *Cong. Globe* 35 (1870)(remarks of Representative Farnsworth).

[3] Act of June 8, 1872, ch. 335, §302, 17 Stat. 323 (1872): "That if any person having devised or intending to devise any scheme or artifice to defraud, or be effected by either opening or intending to open correspondence or communication with any other person (whether resident within or outside of the United States), by means of the post-office establishment of the United States, or by inciting such other person to open communication with the person so devising or intending, shall, in and for executing such scheme or artifice (or attempting so to do), place any letter or packet in any post-office of the United States, or take or receive any therefrom, such person, so misusing the post-office establishment, shall be guilty of a misdemeanor, and shall be punished with a fine of not more than five hundred dollars, with or without such imprisonment, as the court shall direct, not exceeding eighteen calendar months.... "

[4] *McNally v. United States*, 483 U.S. at 357 n.6. The penalty for general violations remained at imprisonment not more than 18 months until the 1909 criminal code revision when it was increased to imprisonment for not more than five years, Act of March 4, 1909, ch. 321, §217, 35 Stat. 1130 (1909). So it stayed until 2002, when it was increased to imprisonment for not more than 20 years, P.L. 107-204, §903(a), 116 Stat. 805 (2002). The penalty enhancement for defrauding a financial institution was added in 1989, P.L. 101-73, §961(i), 103 Stat. 500 (1989), and increased from a maximum of imprisonment for not more than 20 years to its present maximum of imprisonment for not more than 30 years in 1990, P.L. 101-647, §2504(h), 104 Stat. 4861 (1990). The application of the 30-year maximum to disaster related frauds appeared in 2008, P.L. 110-179, §4, 121 Stat. 2257 (2008).

[5] 18 U.S.C. 1346.

[6] P.L. 103-322, §250006, 108 Stat. 2087 (1994).

[7] Act of July 16, 1952, ch. 879, §18(a), 66 Stat. 722 (1952).

[8] H. Rept. 82-388, at 1 (1951)("The general object of the bill is to amend the Criminal Code ... making it a Federal (continued...)

Since its inception, changes in the mail fraud statute have come with corresponding changes in the wire fraud statute in most instances.[9]

Elements

The mail and wire fraud statutes are essentially the same, except for the medium associated with the offense—the mail in the case of mail fraud and wire communication in the case of wire fraud. As a consequence, the interpretation of one is ordinarily considered to apply to the other.[10] In construction of the terms within the two, the courts will frequently abbreviate or adjust their statement of the elements of a violation to focus on the questions at issue before them.[11] As treatment of the individual elements makes clear, however, there seems little dispute that conviction requires the government to prove:

1. the use of either mail or wire communications in the foreseeable furtherance

2. of a scheme to defraud

3. involving a material deception

4. with the intent to deprive another of

5. either property or honest services.

(...continued)

criminal offense to use wire or radio communications as instrumentalities for perpetrating frauds upon the public. In principal it is not dissimilar to the post fraud statute (18 U.S.C. 1341)"); S. Rept. 82-44, at 14 (1951)("This section ... is intended merely to establish for radio a parallel provision now in the law for fraud by mail, so that fraud conducted or intended to be conducted by radio shall be amenable to the same penalties now provided for fraud by means of the mails"); H. Rept. 82-1750, at 22 (1952).

[9] There was no need to amend the wire fraud statute, when commercial carriers were included in the mail fraud statute or when references to the Postal Service were substituted to references to the Post Office, P.L. 103-322, §250006(1), 108 Stat. 2087 (1994); P.L. 91-375, §6(j)(11), 84 Stat. 778 (1970).

[10] *Pasquantino v. United States*, 544 U.S. 349, 355 n.2 (2005)("we have construed identical language in the wire and mail fraud statutes *in pari materia*"), citing, *Neder v. United States*, 527 U.S. 1, 20 (1999) and *Carpenter v. United States*, 484 U.S. 19, 25 and n.6 (1987); see also, *Eclectic Properties East, LLC v. Marcus & Millichap Co.*, 751 F.3d 990, 997 (9th Cir. 2014))(here and elsewhere internal quotation marks and citations have usually been omitted)("The mail and wire fraud statutes are identical except for the particular method used to disseminate the fraud "); *United States v. Kennedy*, 714 F.3d 951, 958 (6th Cir. 2013)("This court has interpreted the mail-fraud and wire-fraud statutes as having essentially the same elements, except for the use of the mail versus the wires"); *United States v. Mullins*, 613 F.3d 1273, 1281 n.2 (10th Cir. 2010) ("[I]nterpretations of the mail fraud statute are, of course, authoritative on questions of wire fraud").

[11] E.g., *United States v. Daniel*, 749 F.3d 608, 613 (7th Cir. 2014)("Wire fraud under §1343 requires the government to prove beyond a reasonable doubt that Daniel: (1) participated in a scheme to defraud, (2) intended to defraud, and (3) used interstate wires in furtherance of the fraudulent scheme. The same elements must be proved to establish mail fraud under §1341, except that the United States mail system, rather than interstate wires, must have been used in furtherance of the fraud for the third element of the scheme"); *United States v. Porter*, 745 F.3d 1035, 1050, 1051 (10th Cir. 2014)("The elements of federal mail fraud as defined in 18 U.S.C. §1341 are (1) a scheme or artifice to defraud or obtain property by means of false or fraudulent pretenses, representations, or promises, (2) an intent to defraud, and (3) use of the mails to execute the scheme.... To convict a defendant of wire fraud under 18 U.S.C. §1343, the government must show (1) a scheme or artifice to defraud or obtain property by means of false or fraudulent pretenses, representations, or promises, (2) an intent to defraud, and (3) use of interstate wire ... communications to execute the scheme"); *United States v. Simpson*, 741 F.3d 539, 547-48 (5th Cir. 2014)("The elements of mail fraud under 18 U.S.C. §1341 are: (1) a scheme to defraud; (2) use of the mails to execute the scheme; and (3) the specific intent to defraud. The elements of wire fraud under 18 U.S.C. §1343 are: (1) a scheme to defraud and (2) use of, or causing the use of, wire communications in furtherance of the scheme").

Use of Mail or Wire Communications

The wire fraud statute applies to anyone who "transmits or causes to be transmitted by wire, radio, or television communication in interstate or foreign commerce any writings ... for the purpose executing [a] ... scheme or artifice."[12] The mail fraud statute is similarly worded and applies to anyone who "... for the purpose of executing [a] ... scheme or artifice ... places in any post office ... or causes to be delivered by mail ... any ... matter."[13]

The statutes require that a mailing or wire communication be in furtherance of a scheme to defraud. It need not be an essential element of the scheme, as long as it "is incident to an essential element of the scheme."[14] A qualifying mailing or communication, standing alone, may be routine, innocent or even self-defeating, because "[t]he relevant question at all times is whether the mailing is part of the execution of the scheme as conceived by the perpetrator at the time, regardless of whether the mailing later, through hindsight, may prove to have been counterproductive."[15] The element may be satisfied by mailings or communications "designed to lull the victim into a false sense of security, postpone inquiries or complaints, or make the transaction less suspect."[16] The element may also be satisfied by mailings or wire communications used to obtain the property which is the object of the fraud.[17]

A defendant need not personally have mailed or wired a communication; it is enough that he "caused" a mailing or transmission of a wire communication in the sense that the mailing or transmission was the reasonable foreseeable consequence of his intended scheme.[18]

Scheme to Defraud

The mail and wire fraud statutes "both prohibit, in pertinent part, 'any scheme or artifice to defraud[,]' or to obtain money or property 'by means of false or fraudulent pretenses, representations, or promises,'"[19] or deprive another of the right to honest services by such means.[20]

---

[12] 18 U.S.C. 1343.

[13] 18 U.S.C. 1341.

[14] *Schmuck v. United States*, 489 U.S. 705, 712 (1989), quoting, *Pereira v. United States*, 347 U.S. 1, 8 (1954); see also, *United States v. Smith*, 749 F.3d 465, 479 (6th Cir. 2014); *United States v. Washington*, 634 F.3d 1183-184 (10th Cir. 2011); *United States v. Jinian*, 725 F.3d 954, 960-61 (9th Cir. 2013).

[15] *Schmuck v. United States*, 489 U.S. at 715, citing by way of example, *Carpenter v. United States*, 484 U.S. 19, 28 (1987); *United States v. Coughlin*, 610 F.3d 89, 98 (D.C.Cir. 2010).

[16] *United States v. Lane*, 474 U.S. 438, 451-52 (1986), quoting, *United States v. Maze*, 414 U.S. 395; 403 (1974); *United States v. Faulkenberry*, 614 F.3d 573, 582 (6th Cir. 2010); *United States v. Phipps*, 595 F.3d 243, 246-47 (5th Cir. 2010).

[17] *United States v. Vilar*, 729 F.3d 62, 95 (2d Cir. 2013)("A scheme to defraud is not complete until the proceeds have been received and use of the mail or wires to obtain the proceeds satisfies the jurisdictional element, which is to say that the jurisdictional element is fulfilled when the defendant uses the mail or wires to convert the money to his own use").

[18] *Pereira v. United States*, 347 U.S. at 8-9 ("Where one does an act with knowledge that the use of the mails will follow in the ordinary course of business, or where such use can reasonably be foreseen, even though not actually intended, then he 'causes' the mails to be used"); *United States v. Porter*, 745 F.3d 1035, 1051 (10th Cir. 2014); *United States v. White*, 737 F.2d 1121, 1129 (7th Cir. 2013); *United States v. Weiss*, 630 F.3d 1263, 1269-270 (10th Cir. 2010); *United States v. Green*, 592 F.3d 1057, 1069-70 (9th Cir. 2010).

[19] *Neder v. United States*, 527 U.S. 1, 20 (1999); *United States v. Smith*, 749 F.3d 465, 477 (6th Cir. 2014)("A scheme to defraud is any plan or course of action by which someone uses false, deceptive, or fraudulent pretenses, (continued...)

From the beginning, Congress intended to reach a wide range of schemes to defraud, and has expanded the concept whenever doubts arose. It added the second prong—obtaining money or property by false pretenses, representations, or promises—after defendants had suggested that the term "scheme to defraud" covered false pretenses concerning present conditions but not representations or promises of future conditions.[21] More recently, it added Section 1346 to make it clear the term "scheme to defraud" encompassed schemes to defraud another of the right to honest services.[22] Even before that adornment, the words were understood to "refer 'to wronging one in his property rights by dishonest methods or schemes,' and 'usually signify the deprivation of something of value by trick, deceit, chicane or overreaching.'"[23]

The statutes condemn schemes to defraud—both the successful and the unsuccessful.[24] Nevertheless, there may be some question whether the statutes reach those schemes designed to deceive the gullible though they could not ensnare the reasonably prudent.[25] It is not uncommon for the courts to declare that to demonstrate a scheme to defraud the government needs to show that the defendant's "communications were reasonably calculated to deceive persons of ordinary prudence and comprehension."[26] One court considered these statements no more than an identification of a point at which the government has satisfied its burden in a particular case, without addressing whether a lesser quantum of evidence might suffice in other cases.[27] In any

---

(...continued)

representations, or promises to deprive someone else of money").

[20] 18 U.S.C. 1346.

[21] *McNally v. United States*, 483 U.S. 350, 356-57 & n.6 (footnote 6 in brackets)("*Durland v. United States*, 161 U.S. 306 (1986), the first case in which this Court construed the meaning of the phrase 'any scheme or artifice to defraud,' held that the phrase is to be interpreted broadly insofar as property rights are concerned. ... the Court rejected the argument that 'the statute reaches only such as cases as, at common law, would come within the definition of false pretenses, in order to make out which there must be a misrepresentation as to some existing fact and not a mere promise as to the future. Instead, it construed the statute to 'include everything designed to defraud by representations as to the past or present, or suggestions and promises as to the future.' ... Congress codified the holding of *Durland* in 1909.... [Prior to *Durland* Congress amended the statute to add language expressly reaching schemes of the period ... . The addition of this language appears to have been nothing more than a reconfirmation of the statute's original purpose in the face of some disagreement among the lower federal courts as to whether the statute should be broadly or narrowly read"].

[22] 18 U.S.C. 1346. The phrase "deprivation of the right to honest services" extends only to bribery and kick-back schemes, *Skilling v. United States*, 561 U.S. 2896, 408-409 (2010); *United States v. Rosen*, 716 F.3d 691, 698 n.3 (2d Cir. 2013).

[23] *McNally v. United States*, 483 U.S. at 358, quoting, *Hammerschmidt v. United States*, 265 U.S. 182, 188 (1924).

[24] *Pasquantino v. United States*, 544 U.S. 349, 371 (2005)("[T]he wire fraud statute punishes the scheme, not its success"); *United States v. Warshak*, 631 F.3d 266, 310 (6th Cir. 2010); *United States v. Lupton*, 620 F.3d 790, 805 (7th Cir. 2010); *United States v. Valencia*, 600 F.3d 389, 429 (5th Cir. 2010).

[25] *United States v. Rodriguez*, 732 F.3d 1299, 1303 (11th Cir. 2013)(acknowledging that "'puffing' or 'sellers' talk' is not a crime under federal fraud statutes").

[26] *United States v. Williams*, 527 F.3d 1235, 1245 (11th Cir. 2008); *Eclectic Properties East, LLC v. Marcus & Millichap Co.*, 751 F.3d 990, 997 (9th Cir. 2014); *United States v. Ciavarella*, 716 F.3d 705, 728 (3d Cir. 2013); but see, *United States v. Corsey*, 723 F.3d 366, 373 (2d Cir. 2013)("In a related context, we have held that a defendant is liable for an objectively absurd lie if a subjectively foolish victim believes it").

[27] *United States v. Svete*, 556 F.3d 1157, 1168-169 (11th Cir. 2009)("Svete and Girardot cite decisions that use the 'ordinary prudence' language as evidence that fraud requires a scheme capable of defrauding the reasonably prudent, but none of the decisions cited by Svete and Girardot overturned a conviction on the ground that the scheme was incapable of deceiving persons of ordinary prudence. The 'ordinary prudence' language was invoked instead to affirm convictions. Two sister circuits have stated that 'ordinary prudence' has a place in the proof of mail fraud, but both held that the jury instructions about materiality were sufficient to establish that the jury had found the fraudulent schemes reliable.... None of these decisions reversed a conviction of mail fraud for failure to instruct the jury that the alleged (continued...)

event, the question may be more clearly present in the context of the defendant's intent and the materiality of deception, matters discussed below.

Materiality

Neither the mail nor the wire fraud statute includes a reference to materiality. Yet materiality is an element of each offense, because at the time of the statutes' enactment, the word "defraud" was understood to "require[] a misrepresentation or concealment of [a] material fact."[28] "[A] statement is material for [mail or] wire fraud purposes only if it has the natural tendency to influence or be capable of influencing the person to whom it was addressed."[29] The deception, however, need not be addressed to the person to be defrauded.[30]

Intent

"Intent to defraud requires a wilful act by the defendant with the specific intent to deceive or cheat, usually for the purpose of getting financial gain for one's self or causing financial loss to another."[31] Under both statutes, intent to defraud requires a willful act by the defendant with the intent to deceive or cheat, usually [, but not necessarily,] for the purpose of getting financial gain for one's self or causing financial loss to another."[32] A defendant has a complete defense if he believes the deceptive statements or promises to be true or otherwise acts in good faith.[33] A defendant has no such defense, however, if he blinds himself to the truth.[34] Nor is it a defense if he intends to deceive but feels his victim will ultimately profit or be unharmed.[35]

(...continued)

scheme had to be capable of deceiving people of ordinary prudence, and none reached the perverse result of insulating criminals who target those least likely to protect themselves").

[28] *Neder v. United States*, 527 U.S. 1, 22-3, 25 (1999); *United States v. Corsey*, 723 F.3d 366, 373 (2d Cir. 2013)("Fraud requires more than deceit. A person can dissemble about many things, but a lie can support a fraud conviction only if it is material, that is, if would affect a reasonable person's evaluation of a proposal"); *United States v. Tum*, 707 F.3d 68, 72 (1st Cir. 2013).

[29] *United States v. Jenkins*, 633 F.3d 788, 802 n.3 (9th Cir. 2011)(parenthetical indications omitted); *United States v. Sharp*, 749 F.3d 1267, 1279 (10th Cir. 2014); *United States v. Seidling*, 737 F.3d 1155, 1160 (7th Cir. 2013); *United States v. Wetherald*, 636 F.3d 1315, 1324 (11th Cir. 2011); *United States v. Radley*, 632 F.3d 177, 185 (5th Cir. 2011); *United States v. Weldon*, 606 F.3d 912, 918 (6th Cir. 2010).

[30] *United States v. Seidling*, 737 F.3d at 1161("[T]his Court does not interpret the mail fraud statute as requiring convergence between the misrepresentations and the defrauded victims"), citing decisions from the First, Fifth, Eighth and Tenth Circuits in accord.

[31] *United States v. White*, 737 F.3d 1121, 1130 (7th Cir. 2013); see also, *United States v. Imo*, 739 F.3d 226, 236 (5th Cir. 2014).

[32] *United States v. Howard*, 619 F.3d 723, 727 (7th Cir. 2010); *United States v. Phipps*, 595 F.3d 243, 245-46 (2010) ("Mail and wire fraud are both specific intent crimes that require the Government to prove that a defendant knew the scheme involved false representations"); *United States v. Stalnaker*, 571 F.3d 428, 436 (5th Cir. 2009).

[33] *United States v. Coughlin*, 610 F.3d 89, 98 (D.C.Cir. 2010); cf., *United States v. Maxwell*, 579 F.3d 1282, 1301 (11th Cir. 2009)("[A]n intent to defraud is not present if the defendant knew that he could not deceive the recipient of his statements").

[34] *United States v. Kennedy*, 714 F.3d 951, 958 (6th Cir. 2013)("[T]he belief or faith that a venture will eventually succeed no matter how impractical or visionary the venture may be is no defense to a charge of fraud"); *United States v. Alston-Graves*, 435 F.3d 331, 336-38 (D.C.Cir. 2006); *United States v. Ramirez*, 574 F.3d 869, 876-77 (7th Cir. 2009); *United States v. Clay*, 618 F.3d 946, 953 (8th Cir. 2010).

[35] *United States v. Hamilton*, 499 F.3d 734, 736-37 (7th Cir. 2007); *United States v. Chavis*, 461 F.3d 1201, 1209 (10th (continued...)

Money, Property, or Honest Services

The mail and wire fraud statutes speak of schemes to defraud or to obtain money or property.[36] They clearly protect against deprivations of tangible property. Their protection of intangibles has not always been as clear. They do protect intangible *property* rights,[37] although they do not apply to certain intangible rights in property that have no value in the hands of the victim of a scheme.[38]

Some time ago, the Supreme Court held in *McNally v. United States* that the protection does not extend to "the intangible right of the citizenry to good government."[39] Soon after *McNally*, Congress enlarged the mail and wire fraud statute coverage to include the intangible right to honest services, by defining the "term 'scheme or artifice to defraud' [to] include[s] a scheme or artifice to deprive another of the intangible right to honest services."[40] Lest the expanded definition be found unconstitutionally vague, the Court in *Skilling v. United States* limited its application to cases of bribery or kickbacks.[41]

Aiding and Abetting, Attempt, and Conspiracy

Attempting or conspiring to commit mail or wire fraud or aiding and abetting the commission of those offenses carries the same penalties as the underlying offense.[42] "In order to aid and abet another to commit a crime it is necessary that a defendant in some sort associate himself with the venture, that he participate in it as in something that he wishes to bring about, that he seek by his action to make it succeed."[43]

(...continued)

Cir. 2006)("A defendant's honest belief that a venture will ultimately succeed does not constitute good faith if, in carrying out the plan, he knowingly uses false representations or pretenses with intent to deceive").

[36] 18 U.S.C. 1341, 1343.

[37] *Carpenter v. United States*, 484 U.S. 19, 25 (1987)("*McNally* did not limit the scope of §1341 to tangible as distinguished from intangible property rights"); see also, *Pasquantino v. United States*, 544 U.S. 349, 356 (2005) ("Canada's right to uncollected excise taxes ... is 'property' in its hands. This right is an entitlement to collect money... Valuable entitlements like these are 'property' as that term ordinarily is employed").

[38] *Cleveland v. United States*, 531 U.S. 12, 20 (2000)(Section "1341 does not reach fraud in obtaining a state or municipal license of the kind here involved, for such a license is not 'property' in the government regulator's hands")

[39] *McNally v. United States*, 483 U.S. 350, 356 (1987).

[40] 18 U.S.C. 1346.

[41] *Skilling v. United States*, 561 U.S. 358, 368 (2010); *United States v. McDonough*, 727 F.3d 143, 152 (1st Cir. 2013); *United States v. Garrido*, 713 F.3d 985, 993-94 (9th Cir. 2013); *United States v. Botti*, 711 F.3d 299, 310 (2d Cir. 2013).

[42] 18 U.S.C. 2(a)("Whoever commits an offense against the United States or aids, abets, counsels, commands, induces or procures its commission, is punishable as a principal"); 18 U.S.C. 1349("Any person who attempts or conspires to commit any offense under this chapter shall be subject to the same penalties as those prescribed rot he offense, the commission of which was the object of the attempt or conspiracy").

[43] *Nye & Nissen v. United States*, 336 U.S. 613, 619 (1949); *United States v. Thum*, 749 F.3d 1143, 1148-149 (9th Cir. 2014); *United States v. Acosta-Colon*, 741 F.3d 179, 208 (1st Cir. 2013); *United States v. Reifler*, 446 F.3d 65, 96-7 (2d Cir. 2006)("[A] defendant may be convicted of aiding and abetting a given crime where the government proves that the underlying crime was committed by a person other than the defendant, that the defendant knew of the crime, and that the defendant acted with the intent to contribute to the success of the underlying crime. To prove that the defendant acted with that specific intent, the government must show that he knew of the crime, but it need not show that he knew all of the details of the crime, so long as the evidence shows that he joined the venture, that he shared in it, and that his efforts contributed towards its success. A defendant may not properly be convicted of aiding and abetting a crime that was completed before his accessorial acts were performed. However, where the crime has more than one stage, the (continued...)

To prove conspiracy to commit mail or wire fraud, the government must establish that (1) two or more persons, directly or indirectly, reached an agreement to devise and execute a scheme to defraud; (2) the defendant knew the unlawful purpose of the agreement; and (3) the defendant joined in the agreement willfully, that is, with the intent to further the unlawful purpose."[44] Most appellate courts do not list an overt act requirement among the elements of the offense, although the Sixth Circuit identifies it as a necessary element.[45] As a general rule, a conspirator is liable for any other offenses that a co-conspirator commits in the foreseeable furtherance of the conspiracy.[46] Such liability, however, extends only until the objectives of the conspiracy have been accomplished or the defendant has withdrawn from the conspiracy.[47]

Where attempt has been made a separate offense, as it has for mail and wire fraud,[48] conviction ordinarily requires that the defendant commit a substantial step towards the completion of the underlying offense with the intent to commit it.[49] It does not, however, require the attempt to have been successful.[50] Unlike conspiracy, a defendant may not be convicted of both the substantive offense and the lesser included crime of attempt to commit it.[51]

(...continued)

defendant may be convicted of aiding and abetting even if he did not learn of the crime at its inception but knowingly assisted at a later stage. The latter principle has been applied to charges of wire fraud, allowing a defendant to be convicted of that offense on an aiding-and-abetting theory even if the wire transmission preceded his conduct, so long as the fraudulent scheme was ongoing at the time of his conduct. In *United States v. Phillips*, for example, the court ruled that the defendant's act of cashing a money order that had been fraudulently wired aided and abetted the wire fraud").

[44] *United States v. Ford*, 558 F.3d 371, 375 (5th Cir. 2009); see also, *United States v. Stimpson*, 741 F.3d 539, 547 (5th Cir. 2014); *United States v. Rodriguez*, 732 F.3d 1299, 1303 (11th Cir. 2013); *United States v. Cole*, 721 F.3d 1016, 1021 (8th Cir. 2013); see generally, CRS Report R41223, *Federal Conspiracy Law: A Brief Overview*, by Charles Doyle.

[45] *United States v. Fishman*, 645 F.3d 1175, 1186 (10th Cir. 2011)("[A] conspiracy to commit wire and/or mail fraud does not require proof an overt act"), citing, *Whitfield v. United States*, 543 U.S. 209 (2005); but see, *United States v. Smith*, 749 F.3d 465, 477 (6th Cir. 2014)(emphasis added)("A conviction for conspiracy to commit mail fraud requires proof beyond a reasonable doubt that the defendant knowingly and willfully joined in an agreement with at least one other person to commit an act of mail [or wire] fraud *and that there was at least one overt act in furtherance of the agreement*"); *United States v. Warshak*, 631 F.3d 266, 308 (6th Cir. 2010).

[46] *Pinkerton v. United States*, 328 U.S. 640, 647 (1946); *United States v. Rodriguez*, 751 F.3d 1244, 1256 (11th Cir. 2014); *United States v. Ortega*, 750 F.3d 1020, 1024 (8th Cir. 2014); *United States v. Ocasio*, 750 F.3d 399, 408-409 (4th Cir. 2014).

[47] *Smith v. United States*, 133 S.Ct. 714, 718 (2013)("Upon joining a criminal conspiracy, a defendant's membership in the ongoing unlawful scheme continues until he withdraws"); see also, *United States v. Ortega*, 750 F.3d 1020, 1024 (8th Cir. 2014)("A defendant is liable for the reasonably foreseeable actions taken by coconspirators in furtherance of the conspiracy unless he affirmatively withdraws from the conspiracy. To establish withdrawal from a conspiracy, the defendant has the burden to demonstrate that he took affirmative action by making a clean breast to the authorities or by communicating his withdrawal in a manner reasonably calculated to reach his coconspirators"); *United States v. Vallone*, 752 F.3d 690, 696-97 (7th Cir. 2014); *United States v. Mandell*, 752 F.3d 544, 552 (2d Cir. 2014).

[48] 18 U.S.C. 1349.

[49] *United States v. Anderson*, 747 F.3d 51, 73 (2d Cir. 2014); *United States v. Muratovic*, 719 F.3d 809, 815 (7th Cir. 2013); *United States v. Gordon*, 710 F.3d 1124, 1150 (10th Cir. 2013).

[50] *Pasquantino v. United States*, 544 U.S. 349, 371 (2005); *United States v. Desposito*, 704 F.3d 221, 231 (2d Cir. 2013); see also, *United States v. Gordon*, 710 F.3d at 1150 ("The fact that further, major steps remain before the crime can be completed does not preclude a finding that the steps already undertaken are substantial").

[51] *United States v. Brooks*, 438 F.3d 1231, 1242 (10th Cir. 2006).

Sentencing

A mail and wire fraud are punishable by imprisonment for not more than 20 years and a fine of not more than $250,000 (not more than $500,000 for organizations), or fine of not more than $1 million and imprisonment for not more than 30 years if the victim is a financial institution or the offense was committed in relation to a natural disaster.[52] Conviction may also result in probation, a term of supervised release, a special assessment, a restitution order, and/or a forfeiture order.

Sentencing Guidelines

Sentencing in federal court begins with the federal Sentencing Guidelines.[53] The Guidelines are essentially a score keeping system. A defendant's ultimate sentence under the Guidelines is determined by reference first to a basic guideline, which sets a base "offense level." Offense levels are then added or subtracted to reflect his prior criminal record as well as the aggravating and mitigating circumstances attending his offense.[54] One of two basic guidelines applies to mail and wire fraud. Section 2C1.1 applies to mail or wire fraud convictions involving corruption of public officials.[55] Section 2B1.1 applies to other mail or wire fraud convictions. Both sections include enhancements based on the amount of loss associated with the fraud.[56]

After all the calculations, the final offense level determines the Guidelines' recommendation concerning probation, imprisonment, and fines. The Guidelines convert final offense levels into 43 sentencing groups, which are in turn each divided into 6 sentences ranges based on the

---

[52] 18 U.S.C. 1341, 1343, 3751. The maximum for both individuals and organizations may be increased to twice the amount of gain or loss associated with the offense, 18 U.S.C. 3571(d). Both mail and wire fraud statutes contain the financial institution and disaster enhancement ("... If the violation occurs in relation to, or involving any benefit authorized, transported, transmitted, transferred, disbursed, or paid in connection with, a presidentially declared major disaster or emergency (as those terms are defined in [s]ection 102 of the Robert T. Stafford Disaster Relief and Emergency Assistance Act (42 U.S.C. 5122)), or affects a financial institution, such person shall be fined not more than $1,000,000 or imprisoned not more than 30 years, or both").

[53] *Gall v. United States*, 552 U.S. 38, 49 (2007)("[A] district should begin all sentencing proceedings by correctly calculating the applicable Guidelines range").

[54] See generally, CRS Report R41696, *How the Federal Sentencing Guidelines Work: An Overview*, by Charles Doyle.

[55] U.S.S.G. §2C1.1 cmt. ("Statutory Provisions: ... 18 U.S.C.... 1341 (if the scheme or artifice to defraud was to deprive another of the intangible right of honest services of a public official) ... 1343 (if the scheme or artifice to defraud was to deprive another of the intangible right of honest services of a public official) ...").

[56] U.S.S.G. §§2B1.1(b)(1); 2C1.1(b)(2). E.g., *United States v. Martinez*, 610 F.3d 1216, 1222 (10th Cir. 2010)("[T]he PSR [(presentence report)]determined Martinez's base offense level was 14 under U.S.S.G. §2C1.1(a)(1), applied a 16-level enhancement under §2B1.1(b)(1) because Martinez was responsible for a loss between $ 1.5 and $ 2.5 million, and applied a 4-level enhancement under §2C1.1(b)(3). When Martinez's base offense level was adjusted three levels for acceptance of responsibility, his total offense level was 31, which when combined with Martinez's criminal history category I, produced a guideline range of 108-135 months"); *United States v. Skys*, 637 F.3d 146, 150 (2d Cir. 2011) ("The PSR's calculation of Sky's advisory-Guidelines offense level began with a base offense level of 7 pursuant to §2B1.1(a)(1); it recommended increases for the following specific offense characteristics: 24 steps pursuant to §2B1.1(b)(1)(M) for an intended loss amount of more than $50 million but not more than $100 million; two steps pursuant to §2B1.1(b)(2)(A) for an offense involving 10 or more, but fewer than 50, victims; and two steps pursuant to §2B1.1(b)(9)(C) for an offense that involved sophisticated means. The PSR also recommended a four-step upward adjustment pursuant to §3B1.1(a) on the ground that Skys was an organizer or leader of criminal activity that involved five or more participants or was otherwise extensive, and a two-step downward adjustment pursuant to §3E1.1(a) for Skys's acceptance of responsibility prior to the imposition of sentence. The total offense level was 37. Given Sky's criminal history category of II, the Guidelines-recommended range of imprisonment was 235 to 293 months").

defendant's criminal history.[57] Thus, for instance, the recommended sentencing range for a first time offender (i.e., one with a category I criminal history) with a final offense level of 15 is imprisonment for between 18 and 24 months.[58] A defendant with the same offense level 15 but with a criminal record placing him in criminal history category VI, would face imprisonment from between 41 and 51 months.[59] The Guidelines also provide offense-level-determined fine ranges for individuals and organizations.[60]

As a general rule, sentencing courts may place a defendant on probation for a term of from 1 to 5 years for any crime punishable by a maximum of term of imprisonment of less than 25 years.[61] The Guidelines, however, recommend "pure" probation, that is probation without any term of incarceration, only with respect to defendants with an offense level of 8 or below, i.e., levels where the sentencing range is between 0 and 6 months.[62]

Once a court has calculated the Guideline recommendations, it must weigh the other statutory factors found in 18 U.S.C. 3553(a) before imposing sentence.[63] Sentences will be upheld on appeal if they are procedural and substantively reasonable. A sentence is reasonable procedurally if it is free of procedural defects, such as a failure to accurately calculate the Guidelines recommendations and to fully explain the reasons for the sentence selected.[64] A sentence is reasonable substantively if it is reasonable in light of circumstances which a case presents.[65]

---

[57] U.S.S.G. ch.5A, Sentencing Table.

[58] *Id.*

[59] *Id.*

[60] U.S.S.G. §§5E1.2, 8C12.4.

[61] 18 U.S.C. 3561, 3581(b).

[62] U.S.S.G. §5B1.1. Probation in conjunction with some combination of incarceration is possible up to offense level 11, U.S.S.G. §5B1.1(a)(2).

[63] 18 U.S.C. §3553(a) ("The court shall impose a sentence sufficient, but not greater than necessary, to comply with the purposes set forth in paragraph (2) of this subsection. The court, in determining the particular sentence to be imposed, shall consider – (1) the nature and circumstances of the offense and the history and characteristics of the defendant; (2) the need for the sentence imposed – (A) to reflect the seriousness of the offense, to promote respect for the law, and to provide just punishment for the offense; (B) to afford adequate deterrence to criminal conduct; (C) to protect the public from further crimes of the defendant; and (D) to provide the defendant with needed educational or vocational training, medical care, or other correctional treatment in the most effective manner; (3) the kinds of sentences available; (4) the kinds of sentence and the sentencing range established for – (A) the applicable category of offense committed by the applicable category of defendant as set forth in the guidelines – (i) issued by the Sentencing Commission pursuant to [s]ection 994(a)(1) of Title 28, United States Code, subject to any amendments made to such guidelines by act of Congress (regardless of whether such amendments have yet to be incorporated by the Sentencing Commission into amendments issued under [s]ection 994(p) of Title 28); and (ii) that, except as provided in [s]ection 3742(g), are in effect on the date the defendant is sentenced; or (B) in the case of a violation of probation or supervised release, the applicable guidelines or policy statements issued by the Sentencing Commission pursuant to [s]ection 994(a)(3) of Title 28, United States Code, taking into account any amendments made to such guidelines or policy statements by act of Congress (regardless of whether such amendments have yet to be incorporated by the Sentencing Commission into amendments issued under [s]ection 994(p) of Title 28); (5) any pertinent policy statement – (A) issued by the Sentencing Commission pursuant to [s]ection 994(a)(2) of Title 28, United States Code, subject to any amendments made to such policy statement by act of Congress (regardless of whether such amendments have yet to be incorporated by the Sentencing Commission into amendments issued under [s]ection 994(p) of Title 28); and (B) that, except as provided in [s]ection 3742(g), is in effect on the date the defendant is sentenced. (6) the need to avoid unwarranted sentence disparities among defendants with similar records who have been found guilty of similar conduct; and (7) the need to provide restitution to any victims of the offense").

[64] *Gall v. United States*, 552 U.S. 38, 51 (2007); *United States v. Smith*, 749 F.3d 465, 484 (6th Cir. 2014)("Procedural reasonableness turns on whether the district court: (1) properly calculated the applicable advisory Guidelines range; (2) considered the other §3553(a) factors as well as the parties' arguments for a sentence outside the Guidelines range; and (continued...)

Supervised Release and Special Assessments

Supervised release is form of parole-like supervision imposed after a term of imprisonment has been served.[66] Although imposition of a term of supervised release is discretionary in mail and wire fraud cases,[67] the Sentencing Guidelines recommend its imposition in all felony cases.[68] The maximum supervised release term for wire and mail fraud generally is three years—five years when the defendant is convicted of the mail or wire fraud against a financial institution that carries a 30-years maximum term of imprisonment.[69] Release will be subject to a number of conditions, violation of which may result in a return to prison for not more than two years (not more than three years if the original crime of conviction carried a 30-year maximum).[70] There are three mandatory conditions: (1) commit no new crimes; (2) allow a DNA sample to be taken; and (3) submit to periodic drug testing.[71] The court may suspend the drug testing condition,[72] although it is under no obligation to do so even though the defendant has no history of drug abuse and drug abuse played no role in the offense.[73]

Most courts will impose a standard series of conditions in addition to the mandatory condition of supervised release.[74] The Sentencing Guidelines recommend that these include the payment of

---

(...continued)

(3) adequately articulated its reasoning for imposing the particular sentence chosen"); *United States v. Schlueter*, 634 F.3d 965, 967 (7th Cir. 2013); *United States v. Christensen*, 732 F.3d 1094, 1100 (9th Cir. 2013); *United States v. Corsey*, 723 F.3d 366, 374 (2d Cir. 2013).

[65] *Gall v. United States*, 552 U.S. at 51; *United States v. Smith*, 749 F.3d at 486 ("For a sentence to be substantively reasonable, it must be proportionate to the seriousness of the circumstances of the offense and offender, and sufficient but not greater than necessary, to comply with the purposes of §3553(a).... A sentence will be found substantively unreasonable when the district court selects a sentence arbitrarily, bases the sentence on impermissible factors, fails to consider relevant sentencing factors, or gives an unreasonable amount of weight to any pertinent factor"); *United States v. Huston*, 744 F.3d 589, 593 (8th Cir. 2014)("A within-range sentence is presumptively [substantively] reasonable"); *United States v. White*, 737 F.3d 1121, 1145 (7th Cir. 2013).

[66] *United States v. Martin*, 363 F.3d 25, 35 n.17 (1st Cir. 2004)("'Supervised release' is a punishment in addition to incarceration, served after completion of a prison term"). See generally, CRS Report RL31653, *Supervised Release: A Brief Sketch of Federal Law*, by Charles Doyle and United States Sentencing Commission, *Federal Offenders Sentenced to Supervised Release* (July 2010), available at http://www.ussc.gov/Research/Research_Publications/ Supervised_Release/20100722_Supervised_Release.pdf.

[67] 18 U.S.C. 3583(a)(emphasis added)("The court, in imposing a sentence to a term of imprisonment for a felony ... *may* include as a part of the sentence as requirement that the defendant be placed on a term of supervised release after imprisonment, except that the court shall include as a part of the sentence a requirement that the defendant be placed on a term of supervised release if such a term is required by statute ... "). There are no statutory provisions requiring a term of supervised release upon conviction for either mail or wire fraud, cf., 18 U.S.C. 1341, 1343.

[68] U.S.S.G. §5D1.1(a)(emphasis added)("The court *shall* order a term of supervised release to follow imprisonment when a sentence of imprisonment of more than one year is imposed, or when required by statute").

[69] 18 U.S.C. 3583(b), 3559(a), 1341, 1343.

[70] 18 U.S.C. 3583(e), 3559(a), 1341, 1343.

[71] 18 U.S.C. 3583(d).

[72] 18 U.S.C. 3583(d), 3563(a)(5).

[73] *United States v. Paul*, 542 F.3d 596, 600-601(7th Cir. 2008)(the sentencing court did not abuse its discretion in imposing the condition upon a defendant convicted of wire fraud who had not history of drug abuse but who did have a history of alcohol abuse and "gambling problems").

[74] U.S.S.G. §5D1.3(a), (c).

any fines, restitution, and special assessments that remain unsatisfied.[75] Defendants convicted of mail or wire fraud must pay a special assessment of $100.[76]

Restitution

Restitution is ordinarily required of those convicted of mail or wire fraud.[77] The victims entitled to restitution include those directly and proximately harmed by the defendant's crime of conviction, and "in the case of an offense that involves as an element a scheme, conspiracy, or patterns of criminal activity"—like mail and wire fraud—"any person directly harmed by the defendant's conduct in the course of the scheme, conspiracy, or pattern."[78]

Forfeiture

Property that constitutes the proceeds of mail or wire fraud is subject to confiscation by the United States.[79] It may be confiscated pursuant to either civil forfeiture or criminal forfeiture procedures. Civil forfeiture proceedings are conducted treating the property itself as the defendant.[80] Criminal forfeiture proceedings are conducted as part of the criminal prosecution of the property owner.[81] The provision authorizing the civil confiscation of property associated with mail or wire fraud is somewhat convoluted:

> The following property is subject to forfeiture to the United States ... (C) Any property, real or personal, which constitutes or is derived from proceeds traceable to ... any offense constituting 'specified unlawful activity' (as defined in Section 1956(c)(7) of this title).... " 18 U.S.C. 981(a)(1)(C). "The term 'specified unlawful activity' means – any act or activity constituting an offense listed in Section 1961(1).... " 18 U.S.C. 1956(c)(7)(A). "(1) As used in this chapter – (1) 'racketeering activity' means ... (B) any which is indictable under any of the following provisions of Title 18, United States Code ... Section 1341 (relating to mail fraud), Section 1343 (relating to wire fraud).... 18 U.S.C. 1961(1)(B).[82]

---

[75] U.S.S.G. §5D1.3(a)(5), (6); see e.g., *United States v. Moschella*,727 F.3d 888, 893-94 (9th Cir. 2013)(upholding payment of restitution as a condition of supervised release).

[76] 18 U.S.C. 3013(a)(2), 3559, 1341, 1343.

[77] 18 U.S.C. 3663A("(a)(1) Notwithstanding any other provision of law, when sentencing a defendant convicted of an offense described in subsection (c), the court shall order ... that the defendant make restitution to the victim of the offense or, if the victim is deceased, to the victim's estate. ... (c)(1) This section shall apply in all sentencing proceedings for convictions of, or plea agreements relating to charges for, any offense ... (A) that is ... (ii) an offense against property under this title, ... including any offense committed by fraud or deceit"); *United States v. Rodriguez*, 751 F.3d 1244, 1261 (11th Cir. 2014); *United States v. Westerfield*, 714 F.3d 480, 489 (7th Cir. 2013); see generally, CRS Report RL34138, *Restitution in Federal Criminal Cases*, by Charles Doyle.

[78] 18 U.S.C. 3663A(a)(2); *United States v. Winans*, 748 F.3d 268, 272-73 (6th Cir. 2014); *United States v. Vilar*, 729 F.3d 62,96-7 (2d Cir. 2013); *United States v. Adetiloye*, 716 F.3d 1030, 1039 (8th Cir. 2013).

[79] *United States v. Smith*, 749 F.3d 465, 488 (6th Cir. 2014)("Criminal forfeiture judgments are mandatory for mail fraud convictions. See 18 U.S.C. 982(A)(2)"); *United States v. Simpson*, 741 F.3d 539, 560 (5th Cir. 2014)("The amount of forfeiture is statutorily defined as any property traceable to gross proceeds of the wire or mail fraud offenses. See 18 U.S.C. 981(a)(1)(D). By statute, the court 'shall order' the forfeiture of the property as part of the sentence if the defendant is found guilty of the offense"); see generally, CRS Report 97-139, *Crime and Forfeiture*, by Charles Doyle.

[80] E.g., 18 U.S.C. 983.

[81] E.g., 18 U.S.C. 982.

[82] *United States v. Taylor*, 582 F.3d 558, 565 (5th Cir. 2009)(rejecting the contention that civil forfeiture under 981(a)(1)(C), 1956(c)(7)(A), and 1961(1) is limited to cases in which a RICO (18 U.S.C. 1962) violation is shown).

Any property subject to civil forfeiture may be confiscated instead using criminal forfeiture procedures, unless Congress has specifically provided otherwise.[83]

A number of defendants, convicted of either mail or wire fraud, have argued to no avail that they should not be held liable for restitution and forfeiture.[84]

Related Criminal Provisions

The mail and wire fraud statutes essentially outlaw dishonesty. Due to their breadth, misconduct that constitutes mail or wire fraud may constitute a violation of one or more other federal criminal statutes as well. This overlap occurs perhaps most often with respect to (1) crimes for which mail or wire fraud are predicate offenses;[85] (2) fraud proscribed under jurisdictional circumstances other than mail or wire use;[86] and (3) honest services fraud in the form of bribery or kick backs.[87]

Predicate Offense Crimes

Some federal crimes have as an element the commission of some other federal offense. The money laundering statute, for example, outlaws laundering the proceeds of various predicate offenses. The racketeering statute outlaws committing predicate offense to operate a racketeering enterprise. Mail and wire fraud are predicate racketeering and money laundering predicate offenses.

RICO

The Racketeering Influenced and Corrupt Organization (RICO) provisions outlaw acquiring or conducting the affairs of an enterprise, engaged in or whose activities affect interstate commerce,

---

[83] 28 U.S.C. 2461(c).

[84] *United States v. Venturella*, 585 F.3d 1013, 1019, 1020 (7th Cir. 2009)("We have rejected the theory that forfeiture and restitution cannot be imposed for the same offense.... Furthermore, outside the rare occasion where the same party stands to benefit from both payments, Biks does not cite to any authority which holds that restitution must be offset by the forfeiture amount; *United States v. Hoffman-Vaile*, 568 F.3d 1335, 1344 (11th Cir. 2009)(rejecting defendant's argument that forfeiture should be reduced because she paid restitution); *United States v. Bright*, 353 F.3d 1114, 1123 (9th Cir. 2004)(rejecting argument that the district court should have 'offset his forfeited funds against his restitution obligation.')"); *United States v. Joseph*, 743 F.3d 1350, 1354 (11th Cir. 2014)("We have held that a defendant is not entitled to offset the amount of restitution owed to a victim by the value of property forfeited to the government, or vice versa, because restitution and forfeiture serve distinct purposes").

[85] E.g. *United States v. Wetherald*, 636 F.3d 1315, 1318 (11th Cir. 2011)(conviction for money laundering, mail and wire fraud, and securities fraud); *United States v. Whitfield*, 590 F.3d 325, 335-36 (5th Cir. 2009)(convicted for racketeering, mail and wire fraud, and federal program bribery).

[86] E.g., *United States v. Jones*, 641 F.3d 706, 709 (6th Cir. 2011)(conviction for mail fraud and health care fraud); *United States v. Ford*, 639 F.3d 718, 719 (6th Cir. 2011)(conviction for wire fraud and false statements in matter within the jurisdiction of a United States agency or department); *United States v. Skys*, 637 F.3d 146, 148 (2d Cir. 2011)(conviction for securities fraud, wire fraud and bank fraud).

[87] E.g., *United States v. Siegelman*, 640 F.3d 1159, 1164 (11th Cir. 2011)(conviction for mail fraud (honest services) and federal program bribery); *United States v. Inzunza*, 638 F.3d 1006, 1012 (9th Cir. 2011)(convicted for wire fraud and extortion under color of official right); *Sotirion v. United States*, 617 F.3d 27, 30 (1st Cir. 2010)(convicted for mail and wire fraud (honest services), racketeering, bribery of public officials, and conspiracy).

---

through loan sharking or the patterned commission of various other predicate offenses.[88] The elements under the more commonly prosecuted conduct prong are: (1) conducting the affairs; (2) of an enterprise; (3) through a pattern; (4) of racketeering activity.[89] "Racketeering activity" means, among other things, any act which is indictable under either the mail or wire fraud statutes.[90] As for pattern, "a person cannot be subjected to the sanctions [of RICO] simply for committing two widely separate and isolated criminal offenses. Instead, the term 'pattern' itself requires the showing of a relationship between the predicates and of the threat of continuing activity. It is this factor of *continuity plus relationship* which combines to produce a pattern."[91]

The pattern of predicate offenses must be used by someone employed by or associated with a qualified enterprise to conduct or participate in its activities. "The 'conduct or participate' element requires a defendant to have some part in directing those" activities.[92] The element is not satisfied unless "one has participated in the operation or management of the enterprise itself."[93] Nevertheless, an "enterprise is operated not just by upper management but also by lower rung participants in the enterprise who are under the direction of upper management."[94]

The enterprise may be either any group of individuals, any legal entity, or any group "associated in fact."[95] An enterprise "associated in fact" "must have at least three structural elements: a purpose, relationships among those associated with the enterprise, and longevity sufficient to permit these associates to pursue the enterprise's purpose."[96] Qualified enterprises are only those that "engaged in, or the activities of which affect, interstate or foreign commerce."[97]

RICO violations are punishable by imprisonment for not more than 20 years and a fine of not more than $250,000 (not more than $500,000 for organizations).[98] The crime is one for which restitution must be ordered when one of the predicate offenses is mail or wire fraud.[99] RICO has one of the first contemporary forfeiture provisions, covering property and interests acquired through RICO violations.[100] As noted earlier, any RICO predicate offense is by virtue of that fact

---

[88] 18 U.S.C. 1962. See generally, CRS Report 96-950, *RICO: A Brief Sketch*, by Charles Doyle.

[89] *In re Classicstar Mare Leasing Litigation*, 727 F.3d 473, 483 (6th Cir. 2013), citing, *Sedima, S.P.R.L. v. Imrex Co., Inc.*, 473 U.S. 479, 496 (1985); *United States v. Nieto*, 721 F.3d 357, 365-66 (5th Cir.2013); *Cruz v. FXDirectDealer, LLC*, 720 F.3d 115, 120 (2d Cir. 2013). A RICO civil cause action also requires a plaintiff to show that the RICO violation resulted in an injury to his business or property, 18 U.S.C. 1964(c); *Cruz v. FXDirectDealer, LLC*, 720 F.3d at 120.

[90] 18 U.S.C. 1961(1)(B); e.g., *United States v. Harris*, 695 F.3d 1125, 129-130 (10th Cir. 2012); *United States v. Teel*, 691 F.3d 578, 581 (5th Cir. 2012).

[91] *H.J., Inc. v. Northwestern Bell Telephone Co.*, 492 U.S. 229, 239 (1989)(emphasis of the Court); see also, *United States v. John-Baptiste*, 747 F.3d 186, 207 (3d Cir. 2014); *United States v. Eiland*, 738 F.3d 338, 360 (D.C.Cir. 2013).

[92] *United States v. Praddy*, 725 F.3d 147, 155 (2d Cir. 2013), quoting, *Reves v. Ernst & Young*, 507 U.S. 170, 183-85 (1993); *Ouwinga v. Benistar 419 Plan Services, Inc.*, 694 F.3d 783, 791-92 (6th Cir. 2012).

[93] *Reves v. Ernst & Young*, 507 U.S. at 183-85.

[94] *Id.; United States v. Burden*, 600 F.3d 204, 219 (2d Cir. 2010).

[95] 18 U.S.C. 1961(4).

[96] *United States v. Eiland*, 738 F.3d at 360, quoting, *Boyle v. United States*, 556 U.S. 938, 946 (2009); *United States v. Harris*, 695 F.3d 1125, 1135 (10th Cir. 2012); *United States v. Applins*, 637 F.3d 59, 73 (2d Cir. 2011).

[97] 18 U.S.C. 1962(c).

[98] 18 U.S.C. 1963(a), 3571.

[99] 18 U.S.C. 3663A(c)(1)(A)(ii); *United States v. Browne*, 505 F.3d 1229, 1281 (11th Cir. 2007); *United States v. Reifler*, 446 F.3d 65, 121 (2d Cir. 2006).

[100] 18 U.S.C. 1963(a), (b).

a money laundering predicate.[101] Victims enjoy a cause of action for treble damages when injured in their business or property by reason of a RICO violation.[102]

Money laundering

Mail and wire fraud are both money laundering predicate offenses.[103] Among other things, the most commonly prosecuted federal money laundering statute, 18 U.S.C. 1956, outlaws knowingly engaging in a financial transaction involving the proceedings of a "specified unlawful activity"(a predicate offense) for the purpose (1) of laundering the such proceeds or (2) of promoting further predicating offenses.[104]

To establish the laundering or concealment offense, the government must establish that "(1) [the] defendant conducted, or attempted to conduct a financial transaction which in any way or degree affected interstate commerce or foreign commerce; (2) the financial transaction involved proceeds of illegal activity; (3) [the] defendant knew the property represented proceeds of some form of unlawful activity; and (4) [the] defendant conducted or attempted to conduct the financial transaction knowing the transaction was designed in whole or in part to conceal or disguise the nature, the location, the source, the ownership or the control of the proceeds of specified unlawful activity."[105]

To prove the promotional offense, "the government must demonstrate that [the defendant]: (1) conducted a financial transaction that involved the proceeds of unlawful activity; (2) knew the property involved was proceeds of unlawful activity; and (3) intended to promote that unlawful activity."[106]

Nothing in the either provision suggests that the defendant must be shown to have committed the predicate offense. Yet, simply establishing that the defendant spent or deposited the proceeds of the predicate offense is not enough without proof of an intent to promote or conceal.[107]

Either offense is punishable by imprisonment for not more than 20 years and a fine of not more than $500,000.[108] Property involved in a transaction in violation of Section 1956 is subject to civil and criminal forfeiture.[109]

---

[101] 18 U.S.C. 1956(c)(7)(A).

[102] 18 U.S.C. 1964(c).

[103] 18 U.S.C. 1956(c)(7)(A), 1961(1)(B).

[104] 18 U.S.C.1956(a)(1). See generally, CRS Report RL33315, *Money Laundering: An Overview of 18 U.S.C. 1956 and Related Federal Criminal Law*, by Charles Doyle.

[105] *United States v. Dvorak*, 617 F.3d 1017, 1021-22 (8th Cir. 2010); see also, *United States v. Valdez*, 726 F.3d 684, 689 (5th Cir. 2013); *United States v. Kivanc*, 714 F.3d 782, 795-96 (4th Cir. 2013); *United States v. Quinones*, 635 F.3d 590, 597 (2d Cir. 2011).

[106] *United States v. Warshak*, 631 F.3d 266, 317 (6th Cir. 2010); see also, *United States v. Valdez*, 726 F.3d at 689; *United States v. Bansal*, 663 F.3d 634, 645 (3d Cir. 2011); *United States v. Quinones*, 635 F.3d 590, 597 (2d Cir. 2011).

[107] *United States v. Naranjo*, 634 F.3d 1198, 1208 (11th Cir. 2011)("The spending of illegal proceeds alone is insufficient to prove concealment money laundering"); *United States v. Faulkenberry*, 614 F.3d 573, 586 (6th Cir. 2010)("What is required, rather, is that concealment be an animating purpose of the transaction"); *United States v. Trejo*, 610 F.3d 308, 314 (5th Cir. 2010)(emphasis of the court)("Instead, there must be evidence of *intentional* promotion").

[108] 18 U.S.C. 1956(a)(1).

Merely depositing the proceeds of a predicate offense does not alone constitute a violation of Section 1956. It is enough for a violation of Section 1957, if more than $10,000 is involved.[110] Section 1957 uses Section 1956's definition of specified unlawful activities.[111] Thus, mail and wire fraud are predicate offenses for purposes of Section 1957.[112] "Section 1957 differs from Section 1956 in two critical respects: It requires that the property have a value greater than $10,000, but it does not require that the defendant know of [the] design to conceal [or promote] aspects of the transaction or that anyone have such a design."[113]

Violations are punishable by imprisonment for not more than 10 years and a fine of not more than $250,000 (not more than $500,000) for organizations.[114] The property involved in a violation is subject to forfeiture under either civil or criminal procedures.[115]

Fraud Under Other Jurisdictional Circumstances

This category includes the offenses that were made federal crimes because they involve fraud against the United States, as well as, the other frauds that share chapter 63 with the mail and wire fraud sections. The most prominent are the proscriptions against defrauding the United States by the submission of false claims, conspiracy to defraud the United States, and material false statements in matters within the jurisdiction of the United States.[116] Bank fraud, health care fraud, securities and commodities fraud, and fraud in foreign labor contracting are all chapter 63 companions of mail and wire fraud.[117]

Defrauding the United States

False claims

Section 287 outlaws the knowing submission of a false claim against the United States.[118] "[T]o sustain a conviction under Section 287, the government must prove: (1) that the defendant presented a false or fraudulent claim against the United States; (2) that the claim was presented to an agency of the United States; and (3) that the defendant knew that the claim was false or fraudulent."[119] The offense carries a sentence of imprisonment for not more than five years and a

---

(...continued)

[109] 18 U.S.C. 981(a)(1)(A); 982(a)(1).

[110] 18 U.S.C. 1957(a)("Whoever, in any of the circumstances set forth in subsection (d)[(including that the offense takes place in the United States)], knowingly engages or attempts to engage in a monetary transaction in criminally derived property of a value greater than $10,000 and is derived from specified unlawful activity, shall be punished as provided in subsection (b)").

[111] 18 U.S.C. 1957(f)(3).

[112] 18 U.S.C. 1957(f)(3), 1956(c)(7)(A), 1961(1)(B).

[113] *United States v. Wetherald*, 636 F.3d 1315, 1325 n.2 (11th Cir. 2011)

[114] 18 U.S.C. 1957(b), 3571.

[115] 18 U.S.C. 981(a)(1)(A), 982(a)(1).

[116] 18 U.S.C. 287, 351, and 1001, respectively.

[117] 18 U.S.C. 1344, 1347, 1348, and 1351, respectively.

[118] 18 U.S.C. 287.

[119] *United States v. Clark*, 577 F.3d 273, 285 (5th Cir. 2009); *United States v. Jirak*, 728 F.3d 806, 811 (8th Cir. 2013).

fine of not more than $250,000 (not more than $500,000 for organizations).[120] The crime is one for which restitution must be ordered.[121] There is no explicit authority for confiscation of property tainted by the offense,[122] but either a private individual or the government may bring a civil action for treble damages.[123] It is neither a RICO nor a money laundering predicate offense.[124]

Conspiracy to defraud the U.S.

The general conspiracy statute has two parts.[125] It outlaws conspiracies to violate the laws of the United States.[126] More relevant here, it also outlaws conspiracies to defraud the United States.[127] To prove conspiracy to defraud the United States, the government must show (1) an agreement between two or more persons, (2) to defraud the United States, and (3) an overt act on the part of one of them in furtherance of the conspiracy.[128] The "fraud covered by the statute reaches any conspiracy for the purpose of impairing, obstructing or defeating the lawful functions of any department of the Government" by "deceit, craft or trickery, or at least by means that are dishonest."[129] Unlike mail and wire fraud, the government need not show that the scheme was designed to deprive another of money, property, or honest services; it is enough that to show that the scheme is designed to obstruct governmental functions.[130]

Conspiracy to defraud the United States is punishable by imprisonment for not more than five years and a fine of not more than $250,000 (not more than $500,000 for organizations).[131] It is neither a RICO nor a money laundering predicate offense.[132] It is an offense for which restitution must be ordered.[133] There is no explicit authority for confiscation of property tainted by the offense.[134]

---

[120] 18 U.S.C. 287, 3571.

[121] 18 U.S.C. 3663A(c)(1)(A)(ii).

[122] Cf., 18 U.S.C. 981, 982.

[123] 31 U.S.C. 3729-3733; see generally, CRS Report R40785, *Qui Tam: The False Claims Act and Related Federal Statutes*, by Charles Doyle.

[124] Cf., 18 U.S.C. 1956(c)(7), 1961(1).

[125] 18 U.S.C. 371; see generally, CRS Report R41223, *Federal Conspiracy Law: A Brief Overview*, by Charles Doyle.

[126] "If two or more persons conspire either *to commit an offense against the United States* or to defraud the United States, or any agency thereof in any manner or for any purpose...." 18 U.S.C. 371(emphasis added).

[127] "If two or more persons conspire either to commit an offense against the United States or *to defraud the United States, or any agency thereof in any manner or for any purpose....* " 18 U.S.C. 371(emphasis added).

[128] *United States v. Coplan*, 703 F.3d 46, 60-61 (2d Cir. 2012); *United States v. Meredith*, 685 F.3d 814, 822 (9th Cir. 2012); *United States v. Whiteford*, 676 F.3d 348, 356 (3d Cir. 2012).

[129] *Hammerschmidt v. United States*, 265 U.S. 182, 188 (1924); *Glasser v. United States*, 315 U.S. 60, 66 (1942); *Tanner v. United States*, 483 U.S. 107, 128 (1987).

[130] *United States v. McKee*, 506 F.3d 225, 238 (3d Cir. 2007); *Hammerschmidt v. United States*, 265 U.S. at 188; *Tanner v. United States*, 483 U.S. at 128.

[131] 18 U.S.C. 371.

[132] Cf., 18 U.S.C. 1961(1), 1956(c)(7).

[133] 18 U.S.C. 3663A(c)(1)(A)(ii).

[134] Cf., 18 U.S.C. 981, 982.

False statements

Section 1001 outlaws knowingly and willfully making a material false statement on a matter within the jurisdiction of the executive, legislative, or judicial branch of the federal government.[135] A matter is material for purposes of Section 1001 when "it has a natural tendency to influence, or is capable of influencing, the decision of" the individual or entity to whom it is addressed.[136] A matter is within the jurisdiction of a federal entity "when it has the power to exercise authority in a particular matter" and "may exist when false statements [are] made to state or local government agencies receiving federal support or subject to federal regulation."[137]

A violation of Section 1001 is punishable by imprisonment for not more than five years and a fine of not more than $250,000 (not more than $500,000 for organizations).[138] It is neither a RICO nor a money laundering predicate offense.[139] It is an offense for which restitution must be ordered.[140] There is no explicit authority for confiscation of property tainted by the offense, unless the offense relates to the activities of various federal financial entities.[141] However, in a situation where the offense involves the submission of a false claim either a private individual or the government may bring a civil action for treble damages.[142]

Fraud Elsewhere in Chapter 63

Chapter 63 contains four other fraud proscriptions in addition to mail and wire fraud: bank fraud, health care fraud, securities and commodities fraud, and fraud in foreign labor contracting.[143] Each relies on a jurisdictional base other than use of the mail or wire communications.

---

[135] 18 U.S.C. 1001; *United States v. Schulte*, 741 F.3d 1141, 1147-148 (10th Cir. 2014); *United States v. White Eagle*, 721 F.3d 1108, 1116 (9th Cir. 2013); *United States v. Castro*, 704 F.3d 125, 139 (3d Cir. 2013).

[136] *United States v. Staad*, 636 F.3d 630, 638 (D.C.Cir. 2011), quoting, *Neder v. United States*, 527 U.S. 1, 6 (1999); *United States v. Griffiths*, 750 F.3d 237, 244 (2d Cir. 2014); *United States v. King*, 735 F.3d 1098, 1107-108 (9th Cir. 2013)("A misstatement need not actually influence the agency decision in order to be material; propensity to influence is enough"); *United States v. Mehanna*, 735 F.3d 32, 54 (1st Cir. 2014).

[137] *United States v. Ford*, 639 F.3d 718, 720 (6th Cir. 2011), quoting, *United States v. Rodgers*, 466 U.S. 475, 479 (1984); see also, *United States v. Jackson*, 608 F.3d 193, 196 (4th Cir. 2010), also quoting, *Rodgers*, 466 U.S. at 479 ("[T]he 'within the jurisdiction' language of the statute merely differentiates the official, or authorized functions of an agency or department from matters that are peripheral to the business of that body").

[138] 18 U.S.C. 1001. It is punishable by imprisonment for not more than eight years if the offense involves international or domestic terrorism as defined in 18 U.S.C. 2331 or if the matter relates to an offense under 18 U.S.C. 1591 (relating to commercial sexual trafficking), ch. 109A (relating to sexual abuse), ch. 109B (relating to sex offender registration), ch. 110 (relating to sexual exploitation of children), or ch. 117 (relating to transportation for illicit sexual purposes).

[139] Cf., 18 U.S.C. 1961(1), 1956(c)(7).

[140] 18 U.S.C. 3663A(c)(1)(A)(ii).

[141] Cf., 18 U.S.C. 981, 982; but see, 18 U.S.C. 981(a)(1)(D)(civil forfeiture)("(a)(1) The following property is subject to forfeiture to the United States ... (D) Any property, real or personal, which represents or is traceable to the gross receipts obtained, directly or indirectly, from a violation of ... (ii) Section 1001 (relating to fraud and false statements) ... if such violation relates to the sale of assets acquired or held by the Resolution Trust Corporation, the Federal Deposit Insurance Corporation, as conservator or receiver for a financial institution, or any other conservator for a financial institution appointed by the Office of the Comptroller of the Currency or the Office of Thrift Supervision or the National Credit Union Administration, as conservator or liquidating agent for a financial institution"); 982(a)(3)(criminal forfeiture)(same).

[142] 31 U.S.C. 3729-3733.

[143] 18 U.S.C. 1344, 1347, 1348, and 1351, respectively.

Bank Fraud

The bank fraud statute outlaws (1) schemes to defraud a federally insured financial institution, and (2) schemes to falsely obtain property from such an institution.[144] To establish the scheme to defraud offense, "the government must prove ... (1) the defendant knowingly executed or attempted to execute a scheme or artifice to defraud a financial institution; (2) the defendant had the intent to defraud a financial institution; and (3) the bank involved was federally insured."[145]

To establish the "falsely obtain" violation, "the government must show that: (1) a scheme existed to obtain money, funds, or credit in the custody or control of a federally insured financial institution; (2) the defendant participated in the scheme by means of a material false pretenses, representations, or promises; and (3) the defendant acted knowingly."[146]

Prosecutors have experienced some difficulty establishing the "financial institution" element of these offenses.[147]

Violation of either offense is punishable by imprisonment for not more than 30 years and a fine of not more than $1 million.[148] Bank fraud is both a RICO and a money laundering predicate

---

[144] 18 U.S.C. 1344 ("Whoever knowingly executes, or attempts to execute, a scheme or artifice – (1) to defraud a financial institution; or (2) to obtain any of the moneys, funds, credits, assets, securities, or other property owned by, or under the custody or control of, a financial institution, by means of false or fraudulent pretenses, representations, or promises; shall be fined not more than $1,000,000 or imprisoned not more than 30 years, or both").

18 U.S.C. 20 ("As used in this title, the term 'financial institution' means – (1) an insured depository institution (as defined in [s]ection 3(c)(2) of the Federal Deposit Insurance Act); (2) a credit union with accounts insured by the National Credit Union Share Insurance Fund; (3) a Federal home loan bank or a member, as defined in [s]ection 2 of the Federal Home Loan Bank Act (12 U.S.C. 1422), of the Federal home loan bank system; (4) a System institution of the Farm Credit System, as defined in [s]ection 5.35(3) of the Farm Credit Act of 1971; (5) a small business investment company, as defined in [s]ection 103 of the Small Business Investment Act of 1958 (15 U.S.C. 662); (6) a depository institution holding company (as defined in [s]ection 3(w)(1) of the Federal Deposit Insurance Act; (7) a Federal Reserve bank or a member bank of the Federal Reserve System; (8) an organization operating under [s]ection 25 or [s]ection 25(a) of the Federal Reserve Act; (9) a branch or agency of a foreign bank (as such terms are defined in paragraphs (1) and (3) of [s]ection 1(b) of the International Banking Act of 1978); or (10) a mortgage lending business (as defined in [s]ection 27 of this title) or any person or entity that makes in whole or in part a federally related mortgage loan as defined in [s]ection 3 of the Real Estate Settlement Procedures Act of 1974").

See generally, *Twenty-Eighth Annual Survey of White Collar Crime; Financial Institution Fraud*, 50 AMERICAN CRIMINAL LAW REVIEW 1023 (2013).

[145] *United States v. Bowling*, 619 F.3d 1175, 1181 (10th Cir. 2010); see also, *United States v. Parker*, 716 F.3d 999, 1008 (7th Cir. 2013); *United States v. Colon-Rodriguez*, 696 F.3d 102, 106 (1st Cir. 2012).

[146] *United States v. Hill*, 643 F.3d 807, 856-57 (11th Cir. 2011); *United States v. Loughrin*, 710 F.3d 1111, 1115-117 (10th Cir. 213); *United States v. Williams*, 390 F.3d 1319, 1324 (11th Cir. 2004); *United States v. Crisci*, 273 F.3d 235, 239-40 (2d Cir. 2001).

[147] See e.g., *United States v. Davis*, 735 F.3d 194, 199, 201-202 (5th Cir. 2013)("In addressing Davis's challenge to the sufficiency of the evidence on the financial-institution element, we set foot on well-trodden terrain. This court has admonished the government to exercise care in satisfying its burden of proving the financial-institution element in prosecuting bank fraud and other bank-related offenses, lest it suffer a reversed conviction on a seeming technicality.... We conclude that the government's evidence was not sufficient to prove a depository institution holding company theory of the financial-institution element.... We do not reach this conclusion lightly, particularly given the government's strong proof as to Davis's conduct relating to other of the elements of the bank-fraud offenses. We can only note, as we have previously, that greater attention to this issue at trial would advance the efficient and fair administration of criminal justice); *United States v. Colon-Rodriguez*, 696 F.3d at 106 ("No rational jury could have concluded that the government proved the [financial institution] element[] beyond a reasonable doubt. As the government has conceded, it offered no evidence that the FSA qualified as a 'financial institution' at the time of the offense conduct in this case.... Accordingly, Colon's conviction ... must be reversed").

---

offense.[149] Conviction also requires an order for victim restitution.[150] Property constituting the proceeds of a violation is subject to forfeiture under either civil or criminal procedure.[151]

Health Care Fraud

The health care fraud proscription in Section 1347 has two prongs as well. It outlaws knowingly and willfully executing or attempting to execute a scheme either (1) to defraud a health care benefit program, or (2) to falsely obtain property from a health care benefit program—in connection with the delivery of, or payment for, health care products or services.[152] Construction of the two prongs mirrors the effort elsewhere, e.g., "To obtain a conviction for health care fraud under 18 U.S.C. Section 1347, the Government is required to prove beyond a reasonable doubt that [the defendant]: (1) knowingly devised a scheme or artifice to defraud a health care benefit program in connection with the delivery of or payment for health care benefits, items, or services; (2) executed or attempted to execute this scheme or artifice to defraud; and (3) acted with intent to defraud."[153] The intent element, however, is a little different. Conviction requires a knowing and willful intent. "To establish knowledge and willfulness, the Government must prove that the defendant acted with knowledge that his conduct was unlawful,"[154] but it need show that the defendant knew of or intended to violation Section 1347 specifically.[155]

Section 1347's penalty structure is also somewhat distinctive. General violations are punishable by imprisonment for not more than 10 years and fines of not more than $250,000.[156] Should serious bodily injury result, however, the maximum penalty is increased to imprisonment for not more than 20 years; should death result the maximum penalty is imprisonment for life or any term of years.[157] Section 1347 offenses are neither money laundering nor RICO predicate offenses.[158] They do entitle the government to restitution,[159] but not to forfeiture of any tainted property.[160]

(...continued)

[148] 18 U.S.C. 1344.

[149] 18 U.S.C. 1961(1), 1956(c)(7)(A).

[150] 18 U.S.C. 3663A(c)(1)(A)(ii).

[151] 18 U.S.C. 981(a)(1)(C), 982(a)(2)(A).

[152] 18 U.S.C. 1347(a); *United States v. Willett*, 751 F.3d 335, 339 (5th Cir. 2014).

[153] *United States v. Martinez*, 588 F.3d 301, 314 (6th Cir. 2009).

[154] *United States v. Rufai*, 732 F.3d 1175, 1190 (10th Cir. 2013).

[155] 18 U.S.C. 1347(b); *United States v. Imo*, 739 F.3d 226, 236 (5th Cir. 2014).

[156] 18 U.S.C. 1347(a).

[157] *Id.* In such cases, the government must show that the offense was the proximate cause of the injury or death, that is, that the injury or death followed as the foreseeable and nature consequence of the offense, *United States v. Martinez*, 588 F.3d at 317-19.

[158] Cf., 18 U.S.C. 1956(c)(7), 1961(1).

[159] 18 U.S.C. 3663A(c)(1); *United States v. Mateos*, 623 F.3d 1350, 1369-370 (11th Cir. 2010).

[160] Cf., 18 U.S.C. 981, 982, 1347. Nevertheless, the same facts may constitute a violation either the mail or wire fraud statute which would permit forfeiture under either civil or criminal forfeiture procedures, 18 U.S.C. 981(a)(1)(C), 1956(c)(7), 1961(1); 28 U.S.C. 2461(c).

Securities and Commodities Fraud

The securities and commodities fraud prohibition in Section 1348 features the same two pronged approach.[161] It outlaws knowingly executing or attempt to execute a scheme (1) to defraud or (2) to falsely obtain money or property—with respect to commodities or securities.[162] "Under Section 1348(1), the Government must provide sufficient evidence to establish that [the defendant] had (1) 'fraudulent intent'; (2) 'a scheme or artifice to defraud'; and (3) 'a nexus with a security.' Alternatively, pursuant to Section 1348(2), the Government can show that [the defendant] executed: (1) a scheme or artifice; (2) 'to obtain, by means of false or fraudulent pretenses, representations, or promises, any money or property;' while possessing (3) fraudulent intent.... " Moreover, "the Government must also show that the false and misleading statements ... were material."[163]

Offenders face imprisonment for not more than 25 years and fines of not more than $250,000 (not more than $500,000 for organizations).[164] The offense is neither a money laundering nor a RICO predicate offense.[165] Victim restitution must be ordered upon conviction,[166] but forfeiture is not authorized.[167]

Fraud in Foreign Labor Contracting

The recently enacted fraud in foreign labor contracting statute, 18 U.S.C. 1351, provides that

> (a) Work Inside the United States.-Whoever knowingly and with intent to defraud recruits, solicits, or hires a person outside the United States or causes another person to recruit, solicit, or hire a person outside the United States, or attempts to do so, for purposes of employment in the United States by means of materially false or fraudulent pretenses, representations or promises regarding that employment shall be fined under this title or imprisoned for not more than 5 years, or both.
> (b) Work Outside the United States.-Whoever knowingly and with intent to defraud recruits, solicits, or hires a person outside the United States or causes another person to recruit, solicit, or hire a person outside the United States, or attempts to do so, for purposes of employment performed on a United

---

[161] 18 U.S.C. 1348.

[162] 18 U.S.C. 1348 ("Whoever knowingly executes, or attempts to execute, a scheme or artifice –
(1) to defraud any person in connection with any commodity for future delivery, or any option on a commodity for future delivery, or any security of an issuer with a class of securities registered under [s]ection 12 of the Securities Exchange Act of 1934 or that is required to file reports under [s]ection 15(d) of the Securities Exchange Act of 1934; or
(2) to obtain, by means of false or fraudulent pretenses, representations, or promises, any money or property in connection with the purchase or sale of any commodity for future delivery, or any option on a commodity for future delivery, or any security of an issuer with a class of securities registered under [s]ection 12 of the Securities Exchange Act of 1934 or that is required to file reports under [s]ection 15(d) of the Securities Exchange Act of 1934;
shall be fined under this title, or imprisoned not more than 25 years, or both").

[163] *United States v. Hatfield*, 724 F.Supp.2d 321, 324 (E.D.N.Y. 2010); see also, *United States v. Mahaffy*, 693 F.3d 113, 125 (2d Cir. 2012)("False representations or material omissions are not required for a conviction under §1348(1). See e.g., *United States v. Motz*, 652 F.Supp.2d 284, 294 (E.D.N.Y. 2009)(identifying elements of securities fraud under §1348(1) as (1) fraudulent intent, (2) scheme or artifice to defraud, and (3) nexus with a security) "); *United States v. Motz*, 652 F.Supp.2d at 296("The parties agree that because the text and legislative history of 18 U.S.C. §1348 clearly establish that it was modeled on the mail and wire fraud statutes, the Court's analysis should be guided by the case law construing those statutes").

[164] 18 U.S.C. 1348.

[165] Cf., 18 U.S.C. 1961(1), 1956(c)(7).

[166] 18 U.S.C. 3663A(c)(1)(A)(ii).

[167] Cf., 18 U.S.C. 1348, 981, 982.

States Government contract performed outside the United States, or on a United States military installation or mission outside the United States or other property or premises outside the United States owned or controlled by the United States Government, by means of materially false or fraudulent pretenses, representations, or promises regarding that employment, shall be fined under this title or imprisoned for not more than 5 years, or both.

The offense is a RICO predicate offense and consequently a money laundering predicate offense as well.[168] A restitution order is required at sentencing,[169] but forfeiture is not authorized.[170]

Honest Services Fraud Elsewhere

After *Skilling*, honest services mail and wire fraud consists of bribery and kickback schemes furthered by use of the mail or wire communications. Mail and wire fraud aside, the principal bribery and kickback statutes include 18 U.S.C. 201 (bribery of public officials), 666 (bribery relating to federal programs), 1951 (extortion under color of official right); 15 U.S.C 78dd-1 to 78dd-3 (foreign corrupt practices); and 42 U.S.C. 1320a-7b (Medicare/Medicaid anti-kickback).

Bribery of Public Officials

Conviction for violation of Section 201 "requires a showing that something of value was corruptly ... offered or promised to a public official ... or corruptly ... sought ... or agreed to be received by a public official with intent ... to influence any official act ... or in return for 'being influenced in the performance of any official act.'"[171]

The hallmark of the offense is a corrupt quid pro quo, "a specific intent to give or receive something of value in exchange for an official act."[172] The public officials covered include federal officers and employees, those of the District of Columbia, and those who perform tasks for or on behalf the United States or any its departments or agencies.[173] The official acts that constitute the objective of the corrupt bargain include any decision or action relating to any matter coming before an individual in his official capacity.[174]

Section 201 punishes bribery with imprisonment for up to 15 years, a fine of up to $250,000 (up to $500,000 for an organization), and disqualification from future federal office or employment.[175] Section 201 is a RICO predicate offense and consequently also a money

---

[168] 18 U.S.C. 1961(1)(B), 1956(c)(7)(A).

[169] 18 U.S.C. 3663A(c)(1)(A)(ii).

[170] Cf., 18 U.S.C. 1351, 981, 982.

[171] *United States v. Sun Diamond Growers*, 526 U.S. 398, 404 (1999); *United States v. Whitfield*, 590 F.3d 325, 348 (9th Cir. 2009); *United States v. Harvey*, 532 F.3d 326, 334-35 (4th Cir. 2008).

[172] *United States v. Sun Diamond Growers*, 526 U.S. at 404; *United States v. Jefferson*, 674 F.3d 332, 358 (4th Cir. 2012); *United States v. Bahel*, 662 F.3d 610, 635 (2d Cir. 2011).

[173] 18 U.S.C. 201(a)(1); *Dixon v. United States*, 465 U.S. 482, 496 (1984); *United States v. Franco*, 632 F.3d 880, 884 (5th Cir. 2011).

[174] 18 U.S.C. 201(a)(3); *United States v. Sun Diamond Growers*, 526 U.S. at 404; *United States v. Ozcelik*, 527 F.3d 88, 96-7 (3d Cir. 2008).

[175] 18 U.S.C. 201(b), 3571.

laundering predicate offense.[176] The proceeds of a bribe in violation of Section 201 are subject to forfeiture under either civil or criminal procedure.[177]

Bribery Related to Federal Programs

Section 666 outlaws bribes offered to, or solicited by, agents of any state, local, tribal, or private entity—that receives more than $10,000 in federal benefits—in relation to a transaction of $5,000 or more.[178] Agents are statutorily defined as "person[s] authorized to act on behalf of another person or a government and, in the case of an organization or government, includes a servant or employee, and a partner, director, officer, manager, and representative."[179] "Where the bribe-giver receives an intangible benefit, the bribe amount may be used as a proxy to stand for the value of the business or transaction."[180] The circuits appear divided over whether the government must establish a quid pro quo as in a Section 201 bribery case.[181] The government, however, need not establish that the tainted transaction involves federal funds.[182]

Violations of Section 666 are punishable by imprisonment for not more than 10 years and a fine of not more than $250,000 (not more than $500,000 for organizations).[183] Section 666 offenses are money laundering predicate offenses.[184] Section 666 offenses are not among the RICO federal predicate offenses, although bribery in violation of state felony laws is a RICO predicate offense.[185] The proceeds of a bribe in violation of Section 666 are subject to forfeiture under either civil or criminal procedure.[186]

---

[176] 18 U.S.C. 1961(1)(B), 1956(c)(7)(A).

[177] 18 U.S.C. 981(a)(1)(C), 1956(c)(7)(A); 28 U.S.C. 2461(c).

[178] 18 U.S.C. 666 ("(a) Whoever, if the circumstance described in subsection (b) of this section exists - (1) being an agent of an organization, or of a State, local, or Indian tribal government, or any agency thereof ... (B) corruptly solicits ... or accepts ... anything of value from any person, intending to be influenced or rewarded in connection with any business, transaction, or series of transactions of such organization, government, or agency involving any thing of value of $5,000 or more ... [or corruptly offers a thing of value to any such agent for any such purposes and in relation to such matters] shall be fined under this title, imprisoned not more than 10 years, or both.
  "(b) The circumstance referred to in subsection (a) of this section is that the organization, government, or agency receives, in any one year period, benefits in excess of $10,000 under a Federal program involving a grant, contract, subsidy, loan, guarantee, insurance, or other form of Federal assistance ...").

[179] 18 U.S.C. 666(d)(1).

[180] *United States v. Townsend*, 630 F.3d 1003, 1011 (11th Cir. 2011).

[181] *United States v. McNair*, 605 F.3d 1152, 1189 (11th Cir. 2010)("In concluding §666 does not require a specific *quid pro quo*, we align ourselves with the Sixth and Seventh Circuits. See, *United States v. Abbey*, 560 F.3d 513, 520 (6th Cir.... 2009) ... *United States v. Gee*, 432 F.3d 713, 714-15 (7th Cir. 2005)"); *United States v. Shoemaker*, 746 F.3d 614, 623 (5th Cir. 2014)("To the extent that the district court concluded that proof of an actual *quid pro quo* was necessary to sustain the convictions, it erred as a matter of law"); but see, *United States v. Redzic*, 627 F.3d 683, 692 (8th Cir. 2010)("To prove the payment of an illegal bribe, the government must present evidence of a quid pro quo, but an illegal bribe may be paid with the intent to influence a general course of conduct. It was not necessary for the government to link any particular payment to any particular action ... "); *United States v. Jennings*, 160 F.3d 1006, 1014 (4th Cir. 1998); cf., *United States v. Ganim*, 510 F.3d 134, 141-42 (2d Cir. 2007).

[182] *Sabri v. United States*, 541 U.S. 600, 605 (2004); *United States v. Brown*, 727 F.3d 329, 338 (5th Cir. 2013).

[183] 18 U.S.C. 666(a), 3571.

[184] 18 U.S.C. 1956(c)(7)(D).

[185] 18 U.S.C. 1961(1).

[186] 18 U.S.C. 981(a)(1)(C), 1956(c)(7)(A); 28 U.S.C. 2461(c).

Hobbs Act

The Hobbs Act, 18 U.S.C. 1951, outlaws obtaining the property of another under "color of official right," in a manner that has an effect on interstate commerce.[187] Conviction requires the government to prove that the defendant: "(1) was a government official; (2) who accepted property to which she was not entitled; (3) knowing that she was not entitled to the property; and (4) knowing that the payment was given in return for officials acts: (5) which had at least a de minimis effect on commerce."[188] Conviction does not require that the public official sought or induced payment, "the government need only show that a public official has obtained a payment to which he was not entitled, knowing that the payment was made in return for official acts."[189]

Hobbs Act violations are punishable by imprisonment for not more than 20 years and a fine of not more than $250,000 (not more than $500,000 for an organization).[190] Hobbs Act violations are RICO predicate offenses and thus money laundering predicates as well.[191] The proceeds of a Hobbs Act violation are subject to forfeiture under either civil or criminal procedure.[192]

Foreign Corrupt Practices

The bribery provisions of the Foreign Corrupt Practices Act are three: 15 U.S.C. 78dd-1(trade practices by issuers), 78dd-2 (trade practices by domestic concerns), 78dd-3 (trade practices by others within the United States).[193] Other than the class of potential defendants, the elements of the three are comparable. They "make[] it a crime to: (1) willfully; (2) make use of the mail or any means or instrumentality of interstate commerce; (3) corruptly; (4) in furtherance of an offer, payment, promise to pay, or authorization of the payment of any money, or offer, gift, promise to give, or authorization of the giving of anything of value to; (5) any foreign official; (6) for purposes of [either] influencing any act or decision of such foreign official in his official capacity [or] inducing such foreign official to do or omit to do any act in violation of the lawful duty of such official [or] securing any improper advantage; (7) in order to assist such [corporation] in obtaining or retaining business for or with, or directing business to, any person."[194]

---

[187] 18 U.S.C. 1951("(a) Whoever in any way or degree obstructs, delays, or affects commerce or the movement of any article or commodity in commerce, by ... extortion or attempts or conspires so to do ... shall be fined under this title or imprisoned not more than twenty years, or both. (b) As used in this section ... (2) The term 'extortion' means the obtaining of property from another, with his consent, induced by wrongful use of actual or threatened force, violence, or fear, or under color of official right ...").

[188] *United States v. Kincaid-Chauncey*, 556 F.3d 923, 936 (9th Cir. 2009), citing, *Evans v. United States*, 504 U.S. 255, 268 (1992); *United States v. Turner*, 684 F.3d 244, 253-56 (1st Cir. 2012).

[189] *Evans v. United States*, 504 U.S. at 268; *United States v. Ocasio*, 750 F.3d 399, 409 (4th Cir. 2014); *United States v. Kalb*, 750 F.3d 1001, 1004 (8th Cir. 2014).

[190] 18 U.S.C. 1951, 3571.

[191] 18 U.S.C. 1961(1)(B), 1956(c)(7)(A).

[192] 18 U.S.C. 981(a)(1)(C), 1956(c)(7)(A); 28 U.S.C. 2461(c).

[193] See generally, CRS Report R41466, *Foreign Corrupt Practices Act (FCPA): Congressional Interest and Executive Enforcement*, by Michael V. Seitzinger.

[194] *United States v. Kay*, 513 F.3d 432, 439-40 (5th Cir. 2007); see also, *United States v. Esquenazi*, 752 F.3d 912, 915 (11th Cir. 2014).

None of the three proscriptions apply to payments "to expedite or to secure the performance of a routine governmental action,"[195] and each affords defendants an affirmative defense for payments that are lawful under the applicable foreign law or regulation.[196]

Violations are punishable by imprisonment for not more than five years and by a fine of not more than $100,000 (not more than $2 million for organizations).[197] Foreign Corrupt Practices Act violations are not RICO predicate offenses,[198] but they are money laundering predicates.[199] The proceeds of a violation are subject to forfeiture under either civil or criminal procedure.[200]

Medicare Kickbacks

The Medicare/Medicaid kickback prohibition in 42 U.S.C. 1320a-7b(b)[201] outlaws "knowingly and willfully [offering or paying], soliciting [or] receiving, any remuneration (including any kickback) ... to induce the referral of[, or the purchase with respect to] Medicare [or] Medicaid beneficiaries ... any item or service for which payment may be made in whole or in part under the Medicare [or] Medicaid programs.... 42 U.S.C Section 1320a-7b(b)[(1),](2)."[202]

Violations are punishable by imprisonment for not more than five years and by a fine of not more than $25,000. Section 1320a-7b kickback violations are money laundering, but not RICO, predicate offenses.[203] The proceeds of a violation are subject to forfeiture under either civil or criminal procedure.[204]

---

[195] 15 U.S.C. 78dd-1(b), 78dd-2(b), 78dd-3(b).

[196] 15 U.S.C. 78dd-1(c), 78dd-2(c), 78dd-3(c).

[197] 15 U.S.C. 78dd-2(g), 78dd-3(e), 78ff(c).

[198] Cf., 18 U.S.C. 1961(1).

[199] 18 U.S.C. 1956(c)(7)(D).

[200] 18 U.S.C. 981(a)(1)(C), 1956(c)(7)(D); 28 U.S.C. 2461(c).

[201] See generally, CRS Report RS22743, *Health Care Fraud and Abuse Laws Affecting Medicare and Medicaid: An Overview* , by Jennifer A. Staman.

[202] *United States v. Mauska*, 557 F.3d 219, 226 (5th Cir. 2009); see also, *United States v. Vernon*, 723 F.3d 1234 (11th Cir. 2013). 42 U.S.C. 1320a-7b provides: "(1) Whoever knowingly and willfully solicits or receives any remuneration (including any kickback, bribe, or rebate) directly or indirectly, overtly or covertly, in cash or in kind – (A) in return for referring an individual to a person for the furnishing or arranging for the furnishing of any item or service for which payment may be made in whole or in part under a Federal health care program, or (B) in return for purchasing, leasing, ordering, or arranging for or recommending purchasing, leasing, or ordering any good, facility, service, or item for which payment may be made in whole or in part under a Federal health care program.... (2) Whoever knowingly and willfully offers or pays any remuneration (including any kickback, bribe, or rebate) directly or indirectly, overtly or covertly, in cash or in kind to any person to induce such person – (A) to refer an individual to a person for the furnishing or arranging for the furnishing of any item or service for which payment may be made in whole or in part under a Federal health care program, or (B) to purchase, lease, order, or arrange for or recommend purchasing, leasing, or ordering any good, facility, service, or item for which payment may be made in whole or in part under a Federal health care program, shall be guilty of a felony and upon conviction thereof, shall be fined not more than $25,000 or imprisoned for not more than five years, or both."

[203] 18 U.S.C. 1956(c)(7)(E), 24(a)(1), 1961(1).

[204] 18 U.S.C. 981(a)(1)(C), 1956(c)(7)(E); 28 U.S.C. 2461(c).

Appendix. Mail and Wire Fraud Statutes

18 U.S.C. 1341. Frauds and swindles (text)

Whoever, having devised or intending to devise any scheme or artifice to defraud, or for obtaining money or property by means of false or fraudulent pretenses, representations, or promises, or to sell, dispose of, loan, exchange, alter, give away, distribute, supply, or furnish or procure for unlawful use any counterfeit or spurious coin, obligation, security, or other article, or anything represented to be or intimated or held out to be such counterfeit or spurious article, for the purpose of executing such scheme or artifice or attempting so to do, places in any post office or authorized depository for mail matter, any matter or thing whatever to be sent or delivered by the Postal Service, or deposits or causes to be deposited any matter or thing whatever to be sent or delivered by any private or commercial interstate carrier, or takes or receives therefrom, any such matter or thing, or knowingly causes to be delivered by mail or such carrier according to the direction thereon, or at the place at which it is directed to be delivered by the person to whom it is addressed, any such matter or thing, shall be fined under this title or imprisoned not more than 20 years, or both. If the violation occurs in relation to, or involving any benefit authorized, transported, transmitted, transferred, disbursed, or paid in connection with, a presidentially declared major disaster or emergency (as those terms are defined in Section 102 of the Robert T. Stafford Disaster Relief and Emergency Assistance Act (42 U.S.C. 5122)), or affects a financial institution, such person shall be fined not more than $1,000,000 or imprisoned not more than 30 years, or both.

18 U.S.C. 1343. Fraud by wire, radio, or television (text)

Whoever, having devised or intending to devise any scheme or artifice to defraud, or for obtaining money or property by means of false or fraudulent pretenses, representations, or promises, transmits or causes to be transmitted by means of wire, radio, or television communication in interstate or foreign commerce, any writings, signs, signals, pictures, or sounds for the purpose of executing such scheme or artifice, shall be fined under this title or imprisoned not more than 20 years, or both. If the violation occurs in relation to, or involving any benefit authorized, transported, transmitted, transferred, disbursed, or paid in connection with, a presidentially declared major disaster or emergency (as those terms are defined in Section 102 of the Robert T. Stafford Disaster Relief and Emergency Assistance Act (42 U.S.C. 5122)), or affects a financial institution, such person shall be fined not more than $1,000,000 or imprisoned not more than 30 years, or both.

Author Contact Information

Charles Doyle
Senior Specialist in American Public Law
cdoyle@crs.loc.gov, 7-6968

www.ingramcontent.com/pod-product-compliance
Lightning Source LLC
Chambersburg PA
CBHW080759290526
45790CB00008B/3510